Crevice: where the light filters through

Edizza Marie Austria

BookLeaf Publishing

India | USA | UK

Presentation by *BookLeaf Publishing*

Web: www.bookleafpub.com

E-mail: info@bookleafpub.com

ISBN: 9789360940621

First edition 2024

*To you who find solace, joy, affirmation,
and reflection in the beauty of words.*

*May this collection resonate with your
heart and soul and bring in the light you've
been searching for.*

ACKNOWLEDGEMENT

This book was completed as a result of the impulsive call to action I felt in my pursuit to be a published writer. I thank Bookleaf Publishing for offering this gracious opportunity.

I am grateful for both my high school and college friends and classmates: I held on to the class prophecy and turned it into reality, somehow.

To all the risks, circumstances, and breakthroughs that gave this book its shape and story.

To the people whom I love, I value you. To the Lord who gave me this gift, I lift up this book for Your glory!

Lastly, I offer my sincerest thanks to those who have finished reading this book. You are loved.

PREFACE

Most of the emotions conveyed in this book were truthfully, involuntarily, excruciatingly, and inevitably felt; some my own, one or two hers, others his, a few theirs, in the end all ours.

Take heart. May you find some answers for all the feelings you carry that you don't always have a word to go with. Take some words suitable for a souvenir. Keepsake. Perhaps, to keep you safe from heartache.

These dark nights will soon fade

It has been dark here, for the longest time, and with no hope for any deliverance. Perhaps, the lesson is of perseverance.

So, I will be patient. I will endure.
It will all make sense.
There is purpose in this turn of events.
Through all of these, I will come out pure.

Look what I have found

I found a love I was willing to sacrifice
everything for, if it meant I could be with them. I
followed it, listening to its echoing cries from
hundreds and thousands of miles away. The love
I poured myself into, never caring if I ended up
empty.

What was wrong with me?

I found a love I was willing to take a chance on,
if it meant I could be less lonely.

Tiny spark

Is it too much to ask for us to be together?

Let us take off our masks and take in all the
pleasure.

A glimmer: I see when you are with me;
of hope that maybe we could share this journey.

Perhaps, the world could be lovely.

Anticipation bled tears

Trickled.

Slowly.

Dribbled.

Unsteady.

Looking

forward

to what is

ahead

was never

meant to be

easy.

Internal screaming

5

Lament for me.

For I, myself, cannot.

Take

this cup

and let it

pass

from me.

Silently

sobbing

screaming

internally.

It is

too

dark

here —

this is

too

heavy.

Lead me

Fleeting glories

of heroes

in fantasies

terrible plot

of tomorrows

forethought

you led me

a bright star

guiding

dreamy

all is fair in love and war

misleading

you have me fooled

my prayers ridiculed.

I whispered little secrets

Untold stories of bravery and cowardice.

Bottled up desires. Suppressed. Conspires.

You don't need to know what I have been through.

I whispered little secrets.

Regrets I interred.

I inferred — faint resets.

In the hazy throes of despair

Terrifyingly

uncontrolled

weep.

Loud

frustrations

wail.

Painlessly

if possible

chisel out

this beating core.

Silent

premonitions

frail

noxiously.

Improbable

dead-end route.

Unconsoled

overleap

sore.

I took it upon myself

Mistakes.

Nailed.

Hammered me.

The cross

I have

to carry.

Tenacious.

A decision

desired

sinful

as it may

look.

Conscientious.

The initiative

I willingly

took.

Leave me alone

It's a burden.

I am.

It's a dilemma.

There is

a weight

I carry

heavy

unspoken

aching.

Unresolved issues.

Drama.

Perhaps, trauma.

Wounds

yet

no visible

scars.

The same as always,

thinking

too much.

Leave me

in isolation

or

put me

in bars.

How to forgive

It may have happened a little too quick
and been short-lived, so to speak,
but it still did happen.

And for every tear you have shed,
may it not root hate and bloom flowers instead.
Let your heart be gladden.

It was here today and gone tomorrow.
Your love remains, even in sorrow.
And for every memory you cannot yet forget,
may it be cherished deeply with the lessons
beget.

The way to forgiveness lies within you — for
you.

Regression

The thought of having to start over to find a love
and a lover hurts more than I thought it would
ever be.

How could your eyes speak of a love that
engulfs mind, heart, body and soul?
How could your touch feel like apricity
enveloping my heart in a gentle warmth?
How could you love me, learn about me and just
go?
How am I supposed to unlearn all the ways you
showed me, how to love and live without you?

My plants, my neighbors, my kitchen are
wondering what is wrong.
They hear me screaming, glass shattering on the
floor.
My appetite is lost. You are nowhere around.

The thought of having to live life without you is
absurd.

Coming to terms

In trying to come to terms with things,
here is what my heart sings:

It's okay
to have been caused pain
and be
the first to forgive.

That is how I'd like to live.

It's okay
to have been
led on to.

It's okay
to have loved
deeply
and
let go.

It's okay
to have given
parts of you.

Even when

all you felt
was hurt
through
and
through.

It's okay
to have loved
deeply.

Even when
you only have
them
exist in memory.

Lost or found

How do we manage to find each other after we have lost one another?

We make love conquer.

The battle is not between you and me —

but of the ego, the heart, the psyche.

You never lost me, and I never lost you.

If love is what we need, it is love that we pursue.

Mementos

The coffee and the coffeeshop we used to go.

The magnificent pattern of the sky and its hue reminds me of you.

We still share the same sky, and certainly you are looking up too.

The gentle breeze, the waves pushing and pulling on the shore, tell me we are still together;

All the flowers, trees, and birds whisper.

The beating of my heart says we are never really apart.

Light it up

If I could gouge my eyes out to stop it from falling tears, I would.

But what good would that make? So, I won't.

The problem was not the unending tears. It was not even the agony or the pain.

The problem was the dark; the echoes of the past; the recurring thoughts and visions and made up situations.

So, I will break this rib cage open.

Bring in the light.

Illuminate the room.

Intermittent progress

22

Take a deep breath.

Take it as often as you need to.

Oh, the bliss! By realizing that you are no longer sad about something you thought you would never get over.

It no longer hurts you. It is what it is. It is now only a fact.

Queries and speculations

Where do you go when your heart is achingly broken?

What do you do when your flesh is weak?

Who do you run to when no one seems to be there for you?

When do you know the time is right?

Why do you think nobody cares about you, if it causes you to cry?

How do you show up and present a smile when you are bleeding inside?

A glint that shimmered

24

To every person I ever was and ever will be.

I'm grateful to all of you, for not giving up on me.

Grieved. I have attended many funerals of my own ego's death.

I have died. Died again.

And then I rose. With lessons learned and experiences gained.

Gilded glowing radiance

To turn inward within oneself is scary and yet courageous. To attempt confronting instead of evading from our own darkness is strength. To turn outward of oneself and engage with others is vulnerability and bravery.

Allowing light to pass through

Let the light in.

Let it penetrate and permeate through the crevices of your heart.

Even when the wounds you thought were already closed still suddenly open and throw you off guard, let the light in.

It is heartwarming. Beautiful.

To have people who would help open up your heart again.

Darkness may consume, but light overcomes.

Remember the day will soon turn into night.

It is necessary. It is temporary.

A part of life.

Maybe we need to break a little.

To make room for the light to filter through.